REAL WORLD ECONOMICS

Understanding
Budget Deficits
and the
National Debt

**KATHY FURGANG
AND
ADAM FURGANG**

ROSEN
PUBLISHING

New York

Published in 2012 by The Rosen Publishing Group, Inc.
29 East 21st Street, New York, NY 10010

Library of Congress Cataloging-in-Publication Data

Furgang, Kathy.
Understanding budget deficits and the national debt/Kathy and Adam Furgang.—1st ed.
    p. cm.—(Real world economics)
Includes bibliographical references and index.
ISBN 978-1-4488-5570-4 (library binding)
1. Budget deficits—United States—Juvenile literature. 2. Debts, Public—United States—Juvenile literature. 3. United States—Appropriations and expenditures—Juvenile literature. I. Furgang, Adam. II. Title. III. Series.
HJ2051.F87 2012
339.5'230973—dc22

2011016170

Manufactured in China

CPSIA Compliance Information: Batch #W12YA: For further information, contact Rosen Publishing, New York, New York, at 1-800-237-9932.

On the cover: The U.S. National Debt Clock, which hangs above Sixth Avenue in New York City, offers a vivid reminder of just how quickly the United States is spending money that it does not have.

Contents

INTRODUCTION

Take a minute to think about all of the things that you want and need every day. Your basic needs are food, clothing, and shelter. But it would also be nice if you had some video games, sports equipment, books, and music. You may even want some food or clothing that you don't necessarily need to survive, like snack food and high-priced sneakers or designer jeans. It won't be long before you must think about the amount of money needed to pay for all of these things.

You can probably think of good justifications to buy just about anything. Books help you learn. Sports equipment helps you stay fit. Movies or video games keep you entertained. Music downloads keep your spirits up and make you happy. New computer gadgets and mobile devices keep you connected and provide important tools to make your daily life far easier. However, these things can all add up to a lot of money.

It is possible that you may not have enough money to pay for all of the things you want. You may have to make hard choices about what you can afford to buy and what you will have to do without, at least for now.

A family's finances work in a similar way as an individual's. Desired purchases must be balanced against available funds, and expenditures shouldn't exceed income. A nation's finances work in a similar way, too. However, families and nations both must consider the good of the whole group, of all their members. If a family does not have food or shelter, its members will suffer. Similarly, the nation is responsible for all its people and must fund programs to help its citizens survive, thrive, and compete with other nations.

So what happens when a family or government does not have enough money to buy the things that are needed? It may have to borrow money in order to meet short-term needs and

The U.S. National Debt Clock hangs outside a New York City building and continuously tracks the national debt.

then repay the loan in the long term. Spending money that one does not have but is borrowed is known as debt spending. A debt is money that is owed to another person or group after it has been borrowed.

When a family or government cannot pay for all of the things that it needs, it may not be able to pay all of its bills either and may begin falling behind on payments. Because of that it will owe more money next month than it did this month as bills and overdue payments pile up. When one spends more than one actually makes or can pay, a budget deficit is created—one's spending has exceeded the funds that are available to spend.

Living in debt and engaging in deficit spending cause major problems for individuals, families, businesses, and the government. It is not easy to pay back money once you start to owe more and more. So why do people get into debt? Things come up that people cannot pay for right away. A medical emergency or a lost job can make a family fall behind in payments. Damage to facilities or equipment, or the costs of developing new products or opening new stores, can cause a business to go into debt. For a government, the cost of wars and weapon purchases, road improvements, public school programs, social welfare programs, and emergency or humanitarian aid cause the nation to go into debt. Hard economic times make paying back debts even more difficult because less money is raised or earned and cash flows out of the economy.

The U.S. government often engages in deficit spending. That is government spending that goes over the amount taken in through taxes. This has been true since the earliest days of the nation, when the newly independent United States sought to build and strengthen its institutions and defend itself militarily with very little available funds. The Founding Fathers knew they needed to spend money to build the country they were determined to build, even if they didn't have the necessary cash in hand. Alexander Hamilton said, "A national debt, if it is not excessive, will be to us a national blessing." He believed it was a necessary way for the young country to compete and become powerful.

When is a budget deficit too large, however, and when does national debt become excessive? Today, the United States' national debt is more than $15 trillion and is expected to grow to $19.6 trillion by 2015. Budget deficits for 2011–2021 are estimated to top $7 trillion. Most economists and politicians believe that the country's budget deficits and national debt are excessive and that action must be taken by the government to live within its means, just as individuals and families are expected to. This means not spending more money than the government collects in taxes and revenue—it must strive for a balanced budget. The government must also begin paying down its huge debt. Just as a family or business can be ruined by overspending and crushing debts, so, too, can an entire country. And the citizens of that country are ultimately the ones who are made to pay.

CHAPTER ONE

HOW AND WHY THE GOVERNMENT GOES INTO DEBT

The idea of a nation going into debt to fund its programs and operations did not start with the United States. Throughout history, many countries have gone into debt. They were often forced to do this to pay for wars and the armies, weapons, and ammunition needed to fight them. Money must be spent on buying or manufacturing weapons, building forts, feeding and clothing armies, and building the ever-evolving implements of war—bows and arrows, catapults, ships, tanks, jet fighters, bombers, and bombs.

For example, Great Britain and France were involved in the French and Indian War in North America from 1754 to 1763. The war was fought far from home for both parties and cost a lot of money to fight. Great Britain went into great debt to fund the long-distance war. How did Great Britain plan on paying back these debts to its allies and creditors? It became necessary to raise taxes on its citizens to help pay the nation's debts.

WHEN DEBT LED TO REVOLUTION

Great Britain passed its taxes on goods to colonists in the New World. This is one of the reasons why colonists wanted to become a nation of their own. They believed that people who paid taxes should be entitled to representation in Parliament. American colonists, however, did not have a representative in Parliament who could voice their concerns, needs, and desires to the British crown and government. They had no voice in the decision making that affected their own lives, livelihoods, and well-being.

It was this very issue of taxation without representation that led to the American Revolution and won the United States independence from its former mother country. The fight for independence, though successful, incurred some hefty costs. At the time the U.S. Constitution was signed on March 4, 1789, the new nation of the United States was already $75 million in debt. This was a staggering figure for the eighteenth century. A lot of the money was owed to France and Spain, two nations who helped pay for the costs of the war being waged against their long-term enemy, Great Britain.

The Founding Fathers knew that something had to be done about paying off the debt quickly. Otherwise, the debt would be left for future generations to pay off. Thomas Jefferson believed that it was immoral for a country to pass along debt to the next generation. Many rich Americans helped pay off the debt with voluntary contributions, and taxes were instituted as well. By

The British government taxed American colonists to help pay off its debts. The Boston Tea Party and other protests led to the American Revolution. Once the colonies declared independence, the national debt was born along with the new nation.

1835, the entire debt was paid off. This was the only time in the nation's history that the United States was debt-free.

USING DEFICITS AND DEBT TO FIGHT THE GREAT DEPRESSION

The United States has often had to rely on deficit spending and the incurring of debt throughout its history. For example, the Civil War almost bankrupted the country. The costs of the war caused the national debt to pass the $1 billion mark for the first time in history.

By 1913, after various cycles of economic boom and bust and repeated financial panics and banking crises, it became clear that the nation needed an agency to help manage its money supply and oversee banks. As a result, the Federal Reserve was created. This agency also introduced the income tax. The Sixteenth Amendment to the Constitution was added, making it a law that all citizens and companies must pay to the government a certain percentage of their income or revenue.

Taxes became an important way for the government to raise the necessary funds for its programs and services. Before this time, only the richest Americans paid a tax on income. But much more money was able to be raised once most citizens began contributing to the pot. By 1918, more than a billion dollars in federal taxes had been raised for the first time in history. As more jobs were created and more companies were founded and began operating, more taxes were collected.

However, the federal government also had more and more reasons to spend money as the twentieth century continued. World War I sank the country deeper into debt, and then the Great Depression began in 1929. A lot fewer taxes

During the Great Depression, the federal government engaged in deficit spending to create public works and relief agencies like the Works Progress Administration (WPA). The WPA helped create jobs for millions of Americans in need.

were collected over the next decade and a half because many people lost their jobs. Many companies went out of business. The country suffered tremendously during this time, and many Americans became jobless, homeless, and hungry.

The federal government recognized the desperate need of its citizens and tried to do something to protect and sustain them. Through the initiative of President Franklin D. Roosevelt, a package of programs and services known as the New Deal was created. Some of these programs paid Americans to get back to work building public roads, buildings, and parks. New

World War II created the need for even more deficit spending so that weapons could be manufactured. Yet this spending and sharp boost in industrial production also lifted the United States out of the Great Depression after almost fifteen years of suffering.

government agencies were formed that were designed to protect the interests of the elderly, the ill, the unemployed, children, and other groups who require special assistance.

This intervention by the federal government protected its most vulnerable and suffering citizens. Its spending programs were designed to stimulate the dying economy. The New Deal created jobs, helped people survive, and got cash flowing through the economy again during some of the darkest and most desperate years of the nation's history.

The United States wanted to maintain its standing as one of the most powerful nations in the world. The economic devastation of the Great Depression was so great that the country risked losing ground and heading backward in terms of development. To avoid this, the government had to inject money into the economy, launch numerous public works projects, and provide its citizens with the means to obtain both work and food. The nation's most valuable asset was its people, and they needed to be protected and nurtured at all costs. Yet these costs were steep, and the government was forced to engage in deficit spending to meet them.

WAR BONDS TO THE RESCUE

The spending and manufacturing associated with the effort to prepare the United States for its entry into World War II helped end the Great Depression. But this military spending also put the nation into even deeper debt, which stood at $200 billion by war's end. This was the highest debt the country had run up to date.

How did the country pay for such an expensive war and dig out of its debt hole? American citizens themselves helped

BUY WAR BONDS

Much of the debt from World War II was paid off by American citizens who bought war bonds.

by paying down the debt out of their own pockets through the purchasing of government-issued bonds. The federal government would immediately receive the money that citizens paid for the bonds. In return, the government promised to pay citizens back the money in the future with added interest. The government's hope was that at the time the bonds would need to be paid back, the country would be in a better position to pay back the citizen bondholders. In the meantime, it could use the money to pay for the war effort, pay down debt, and fund important public projects. War bonds and other types of bonds are a good way to help a government raise money for desired projects. Americans felt strongly about the war, and millions of people bought bonds to help the government during this difficult time.

By the end of the war, half of the U.S. population, which was eighty-five million people, had bought bonds. The total earned for the war effort through sales of war bonds was $185.7 billion. As a result, the country was able to enter a time of prosperity during the 1950s, with a relatively low debt load.

MAKING A BUDGET

Just like any family, a government has to make a budget to determine how much money it has to spend and decide what that money should be spent on. If a government just spends whatever it wants, whenever it wants, without making sure

17

What Is the Gross National Product?

The gross national product (GNP) is the total value of the goods and services produced in one year by labor and property supplied by the residents of a country. This statistic is important for economists to consider when they look at a country's debt and deficit spending. The GNP gives economists an idea of the country's ability to pay off its debt and get out of deficit spending. The more a country produces in goods and provides in services, the more money its companies and citizens make, and the more revenue the government collects in the form of taxes. The more revenue collected, the sooner deficits can be narrowed (or closed) and debt can be lowered (or even erased).

For example, soon after the Revolutionary War, the nation's debt was 40 percent of its GNP. That amount increased and decreased over the years. By 1992, the country's $4 trillion debt was 64 percent of the GNP. That meant the money the United States owed was more than half of what it could produce in a year. In 2011, the $15 trillion debt was almost 100 percent of the GNP. That means the money the United States owes in debt is about equal to the value of the goods and services it can produce in a year.

there is enough revenue to cover the purchases, the money will quickly run out. Each year, the government makes a detailed plan—the federal budget—to determine how much money it has taken in, how much it plans to spend, what it plans to spend it on, and how much money it will need to borrow (if any) to make these expenditures.

A budget is submitted by the federal government every year to indicate what projected revenues are, how much money will be spent, and where and how it will be spent.

FISCAL YEAR 2012
BUDGET
OF THE U.S. GOVERNMENT

OFFICE OF MANAGEMENT AND BUDGET

BUDGET.GOV

If the government cannot make a budget that balances what is coming in (revenue) with what is being spent, deficit spending and increased debt are the result. As more and more debt piles up year after year, it becomes more difficult to craft a balanced budget in which revenue matches desired expenditures. In 1992, the national debt was almost 70 percent of the total value of all the goods and services the country produced (the gross national product, or GNP). Over the next decade, the country's debt is expected to increase to more than 90 percent of the GNP. It is generally agreed that for sustainable economic health, a nation's debt should be less than half of its GNP.

It should also be remembered that national debt is like personal or household debt. The amount owed does not remain the same as the amount initially borrowed but increases over time due to interest charged on the loan. So debt gets more expensive and grows the longer it remains unpaid. Servicing the debt—or even just paying the interest that has accrued and is owed on the original loan amount—is a major expense that must be budgeted for in its own right. This is another reason why once a government takes on debt, it becomes very hard to get out of it. The costs of debt just keep accruing and adding to the total debt load. Debt can often increase faster than it can be paid back, so the debtor is forever falling behind and losing ground.

CHAPTER TWO

WHERE DOES THE MONEY GO?

What does the nation spend its money on? The first thing that might come to mind is the funding of federal government operations and facilities in Washington, D.C., the nation's capital. Paying government employees, maintaining government buildings, and buying office equipment for the White House, Congress, and all the federal agencies are some of the obvious and mandatory costs that the government must pay every year.

FUNDING GOVERNMENT AGENCIES AND PROGRAMS

In addition to the costs of operating government offices in Washington, there are also defense-related costs. This is the spending associated with homeland security, the military, and intelligence-gathering. This includes, among many other things, the training, housing, clothing, and feeding of soldiers; the maintenance of armed forces facilities; weapons purchases and maintaining; updating and maintaining security equipment at border crossings and in airports; and satellite and cyber-defense technologies. The federal budget also funds the exploration of space, primarily through the National Aeronautics and Space Administration (NASA).

But this is only the beginning. There are many, many more things that the federal government spends money on to the daily benefit of its citizens. The operation of public schools, national parks, national monuments, some museums, public libraries, the postal service, a national weather service, arts programs, and early education and school lunch programs all receive federal funding.

If you look further, you will find that the government provides protection to its citizens in the form of various health and welfare programs. This includes Social Security payments for the elderly and retired, welfare payments for those living in poverty, and unemployment insurance payments for those out of work. Disability insurance goes to people who are injured or disabled in some way and cannot work. Thanks to Medicare and Medicaid, health care costs are reduced for those who are retired, disabled, or have a low

U.S. soldiers collect their gear in Afghanistan's Kandahar Province. In recent years, national defense has made up almost 20 percent of the federal budget.

income. The federal government also provides aid to areas that have been devastated by natural disasters or storms. This disaster assistance helps citizens get back on their feet and repair their communities.

How Does It Add Up?

The following is a breakdown of the proposed federal budget for 2011:

Defense	$928.5 billion
Health Care	$898.0 billion
Pensions	$787.6 billion
Welfare	$464.6 billion
Interest on Debt	$250.7 billion
Education	$140 billion
Other Spending	$170.2 billion
Transportation	$104.2 billion
Protection	$57.3 billion
General Government	$29.0 billion
Total:	**$3.83 trillion**

The U.S. federal deficit for 2011 was estimated to be $1.27 trillion. The national debt was more than $14 trillion. The GNP was around $15 trillion. The federal government was expected to take in about $4.5 trillion in tax revenue. What all of this means is that costs pile up faster than revenue can come in. The 2011 budget would most likely exceed available revenue, thereby adding to the federal budget deficit. In the meantime, the national debt would only grow larger.

The federal budget of the United States is designed to benefit the broadest number of citizens. Since all citizens are paying taxes to support the government, the money spent attempts to satisfy and serve the greatest number of people.

SPENDING BEYOND REVENUE

The government spends a lot of money, but it takes in a lot of money, too. The money that any government organization takes in is called its revenue. The United States gets most of its revenue from its citizens and businesses. In recent years, income taxes from citizens and businesses accounted for at least 55 percent of the federal government's revenue. Another 36 percent came from Social Security taxes. These income and Social Security taxes now amount to more than $2.5 trillion. While this is a lot of money, it is not enough to avoid further deficit spending without drastically reducing the size of the federal budget. This would involve slashing many important and popular government programs that serve the needs of American citizens, particularly the most vulnerable ones.

Over the past forty-five years, the United States has been operating in a budget deficit for all but five of those years. Simply put, this means that the country habitually spends more than it takes in. For the final five years of Bill Clinton's presidency, the federal government operated with a budget surplus. That meant the budget was balanced to the point where more money was being taken in as revenue than was going out as expenditure.

Since the beginning of the twenty-first century, beginning with the administration of President George W. Bush, the United States returned to deficit spending. One major

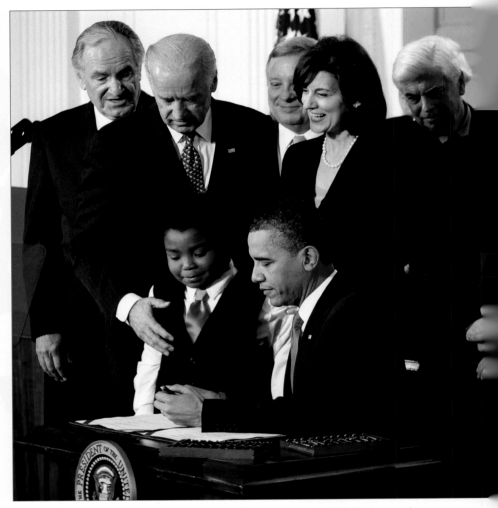

A health insurance reform bill signed into law in 2010 by President Barack Obama is expected to create more deficit spending in the years to come.

cause was the terrorist attacks of September 11, 2001. The U.S. response to these attacks included prolonged military operations in Iraq and Afghanistan, as well as the deployment of expensive homeland security measures and

26

technologies to wage the war on terror domestically.

The federal government must weigh the importance of each funding and policy decision by thinking about its impact on the American people. The idea of protecting the country from further terrorist attacks was weighed against the economic importance of paying down the debt with the help of continued budget surpluses. The security of the nation and its citizens was seen as more important than the eventual economic consequences of a return to deficit spending and a ballooning national debt.

In 2001, the nation's debt was close to $6 trillion. Ten years later, the debt had more than doubled to over $15 trillion. Another government expense that increased government spending and the national debt during this period was the introduction of new health care legislation. In 2010, President Barack Obama introduced a plan designed to extend health coverage to all Americans. It cost trillions of dollars to implement but was designed to help lower the debt in the long run by bringing health care costs down for both individuals and the federal government.

27

What About the States?

The federal government is not the only level of government that engages in deficit spending. Each of the country's fifty states drafts a budget to map out spending on state agencies, institutions, programs, and projects. If a state cannot balance its budget, it goes into deficit spending. Some states have been running budget deficits for many years, similar to the federal government. In 2010, the ten states with the largest budget deficits were California, Oklahoma, Arizona, Illinois, Hawaii, New Jersey, New York, Nevada, Colorado, and Michigan.

Budget deficits translate into big problems for states. In 2010, for example, California had a budget gap of about $20 billion. That caused the state government to make difficult choices that negatively affected virtually everyone. Teachers had to be laid off, some important services could no longer be offered, and state workers had to take pay cuts or be laid off. Since 2010, the economy has been slowly improving, but many states are still deep in a fiscal hole.

THE DANGER OF DEBT

The dangers of a large national debt have long been debated. Many politicians feel that spending is necessary—especially in times of recession—to allow the country to compete internationally and maintain its position as one of the world's leading industrial and technological powers. Others feel the debt that will be passed on to younger generations is not acceptable

28

Working Americans pay part of their income in taxes to the government. When a greater number of people are unemployed, less tax revenue is earned. This usually increases the federal budget deficit and may result in cuts to federal programs.

and will decrease their ability to achieve prosperity as individuals and as a nation. These debates and discussions have been going on since the beginning of the nation's history. For example, Thomas Jefferson felt that it was morally unacceptable for debt to be passed on to future generations. Alexander Hamilton, on the other hand, felt that a manageable debt can allow a country to compete with others. Today's politicians are still faced with the same debate, make the same arguments, and arrive at the same lack of consensus and conclusions.

If the debt becomes more than its government or citizens can manage, taxes may be raised to help pay it down. The higher taxes may be more than many people can afford. For example, some American workers today are already required to pay about 20 percent of their income to the federal government in the form of taxes to help pay for the costs of running the country. However, if the country continues to spend more than it takes in, it will have to borrow more money to cover the resulting budget deficits. As a result, the people will be forced to pay higher and higher percentages of their income to the government to service the ever-increasing debt. This will leave them with less money to pay for their own daily expenses, such as running a home.

The fear of higher taxes and increased debt is making citizens more aware of how the federal government is spending their tax dollars. One of the American people's most powerful ways to influence government decision making and policy is to vote. Ordinary citizens can vote politicians into or out of office if they are dissatisfied with an officeholder's actions, proposals, or policies, including spending decisions and taxation issues.

THE SOCIAL SECURITY COMPLICATION

Social Security payments are a big part of the federal government's revenue pie. The Social Security tax is money that

The U.S. Treasury provides Social Security checks to millions of people each month. These payments represent the largest spending obligation in the federal budget.

workers contribute from their paychecks. In return, when they retire, they will get a monthly payment from the government to use for their daily living expenses. The money contributed does not go into a personalized retirement account for the worker. Instead, the taxes collected from current workers are meant to be paid out to those who are now retired. When current workers retire, the taxes collected from a younger generation of workers will provide their monthly Social Security checks. For example, a twenty-year-old makes a Social Security payment from her paycheck, but it is paid out to a seventy-year-old who is eligible to receive payments.

In the years after Social Security was first introduced during the Great Depression, this system worked fine. More people were working than were retired, so the federal government actually had a Social Security surplus each year. This surplus was often applied to the budget to close or eliminate deficits. But then the "baby boom" generation—the huge number of people who were born between the end of World War II in 1946 and 1964—began to retire. This was the largest generation ever to exist in the United States—seventy-nine million people—and their retirements place a massive burden on the Social Security system. Economists believe that by 2017, the United States will be paying out more in Social Security payments than it will be taking in. These obligatory payments will be adding to the budget deficit and national debt, instead of helping pay for it as in the days of Social Security surplus.

These same baby boomer retirees receiving Social Security payments will also be receiving Medicare payments. This is another cost to the government. Economists have debated what to do about Social Security for many years. Doing away with the system would leave millions of people without the payments they are owed and have been promised. It would also leave the federal government without a large percentage of its tax revenue. Passing the system to a private company to handle (privatization) could run the risk of bad investments or mismanagement, resulting in huge losses and a failure to meet guaranteed payments. There are no easy or surefire solutions to the problem of how to insure continued and adequate funding of Social Security in the future.

CHAPTER THREE

HOW DOES THE GOVERNMENT BORROW MONEY?

Governments at every level—federal, state, and local—can draw up budgets that operate at a deficit. The proposed expenditures are greater than the revenue that has been collected in the form of taxes. Therefore, in order to meet the budget obligations, governments sometimes need to borrow money. But where is the money borrowed from?

THE FEDERAL RESERVE AND MANAGEMENT OF THE MONEY SUPPLY

Like ordinary citizens, when the federal government needs cash, it relies on a bank for help. In this case, it goes to the Federal Reserve. The Federal Reserve, which serves as the central bank of the country, is a federal institution that controls the nation's money supply.

In recessionary periods, the economy is typically starved of cash. The Federal Reserve can increase the money supply and get cash circulating through the economy again by lowering interest rates. Lower interest rates make borrowing money

The U.S. Federal Reserve building in Washington, D.C., serves as the nation's central bank. It controls the nation's money supply, largely through the raising or lowering of interest rates.

cheaper and encourage businesses and governments to begin spending again. This, in turn, stimulates the economy, generates higher tax revenues, and fills the government's coffers, allowing for a paying down of the national debt.

You may wonder why the government does not just print the money it needs to pay off its debts. In theory, the government can print as much money as it wants, but that would cause other problems. Printing more money would cause the currency to be worth less, which is called inflation.

When too much money is circulating in the economy, prices rise and the purchasing power of the dollar—its actual value—goes down. That would mean that a gallon of milk that cost $3 a year ago may now cost $4 or $5. Higher prices mean slow sales and a sluggish economy, which ultimately leads to lower tax revenue and increased debt for the federal government. When too much money is circulating in an economy and inflation is harming economic activity, the Federal Reserve can drain the economy of cash by raising interest rates. The greater expense of borrowing stanches the flow of cash, and the money supply and prices come into better balance.

No matter how bad it seems to be carrying a large debt load, it is even worse to have high inflation. When the currency is worth next to nothing, it takes a lot more money to actually purchase anything of value. It is important for the United States to try to keep the value of the American dollar as high as possible. So instead of printing more money to pay for debt and make up for deficit spending, the Federal Reserve tries to regulate the money supply at optimum levels. Meanwhile, the government seeks to borrow cash from lenders interested in making a profit.

TREASURY SECURITIES AND BONDS

Today, the federal government's deficit spending is no longer financed only by bonds bought by its citizens. The government must also borrow money from foreign countries.

How is that help offered by other countries? Foreign countries buy certificates known as Treasury securities or Treasury bonds. Foreign countries and institutions can buy these. The money they pay for the certificates goes to the U.S. government. The government promises to pay the bonds back within the amount of time stated on the bond. It can often be as long as thirty years before the bond becomes mature and the money is paid back to the investor.

When Spending Is Slashed

If the United States is continuously deficit spending and getting ever deeper into debt, why doesn't it just stop spending entirely? Some politicians recommend ideas similar to this, but the unforeseen consequences could be severe and as bad as those associated with massive debt. The pros and cons must be weighed before any spending is cut.

There are likely many places that spending can be cut easily without affecting the well-being of the majority of American people. But there are many budget cuts that would negatively affect the country in a serious way. What if the military suddenly stopped receiving money to defend the country? What if schools were closed, parks and libraries were shut down, or elderly people stopped receiving payments they rely on to live? What if the unemployed received no aid and quickly lost their homes and could not afford to feed their families? What if the disabled or poor suddenly stopped receiving the money they have relied on for years? Not only would individuals and certain groups be harmed by such sharp cuts, but the social fabric would fray and disintegrate. Everyone would ultimately be negatively impacted, as would the economy.

A severe and sudden end to spending would have devastating effects on the vast majority of ordinary citizens whom the federal government seeks to assist and support. This is why politicians argue over what kind of spending should be cut, what should be decreased, and what should be increased. They are trying to strike just the right balance between fiscal responsibility and the health and well-being of American society and all its members.

The interest on a Treasury bond is often low, so the buyer does not get a huge return on his or her investment. Instead buyers get the security that comes with the knowledge that they are supporting the enterprises of a country and that if that country prospers, the investor will, too. This is the same principle expressed in the proverb, "A rising tide lifts all boats." When a nation is prosperous, anyone doing business in or with that country is likely to become prosperous, too.

The countries that own the greatest amount of U.S. Treasury bonds are China, Japan, the United Kingdom, and various oil-exporting nations. China owns $895 billion in U.S. Treasury bonds, and Japan owns $877 billion. The United Kingdom owns $511 billion, and oil exporters own $210 billion. Having bought U.S. Treasury bonds, these countries are said to "own American debt." They are essentially the nation's creditors (lenders).

What's in It for Them?

Why would these countries be interested in helping the United States pay its bills? They see the United States as important to their own nation's businesses and economic health. China manufactures a lot of goods that the United States buys. If the United States can no longer afford to buy the goods that

China makes, the economy in China will suffer as well. The United States also buys a lot of goods from Japan, and Japan gives the United States money for the same reason. If the United States failed, many other countries would not be far behind.

Today, many products are manufactured outside of the United States. This gives the country less revenue from export sales than it had in previous decades. Purchase of foreign goods by American consumers also bites into the profits of U.S. businesses.

So it is in China and Japan's best interest to make sure that the U.S. economy can continue to perform at a high level. The United Kingdom is a close military ally of the United States, and the two nations rely on each other for mutual defense and the protection of shared national interests around the globe. Oil-exporting nations need the United States to continue to be able to buy their precious commodity as well, given that America is one of the largest oil-importing and oil-consuming nations in the world. The United States imports hundreds of billions of dollars worth of foreign oil every year.

WHAT ARE THE RISKS OF FOREIGN AID?

When the United States sells Treasury bonds to countries or corporations around the world, there are some consequences. For example, a country such as China pays a lot of money to the United States, but what if it does something that violates the policies or principles of the United States? The United States may be less likely to react in the way it would like to because it knows that China is a financial ally, a major lender, and a controller of American debt.

The fact that China provides it with so much money also puts pressure on the United States to import and purchase Chinese goods, rather than those of another country or American-made products (even if the latter are superior in quality or price). A lender-borrower relationship affects the debtor nation's policies as well as its interactions with the creditor nation. The debtor nation is less free to operate as it wishes, is less autonomous, than it would be if it were debt-free.

Hong Kong pro-democracy legislators protest China's arrest and imprisonment of political dissident and literary critic Liu Xiaobo. Because China owns so much American debt, the U.S. government is forced to tread lightly around the issue of that nation's possible human rights abuses.

Another risk in accepting a lot of money from foreign creditors is that the United States must eventually pay back a very large amount of money with interest. If the United States is unable to do that when asked or required, the relationship with the creditor is put at risk. That nation may stop lending money, or its alliance with the United States may be strained or even ended.

One more risk that must be considered is that the more the United States needs to borrow from foreign creditors, the less desirable the country looks to these investors. The reason China and Japan put so much money into Treasury bonds is because they feel that the United States is a valuable asset to the world and the country can help them succeed as well. But the more the United States needs to borrow, the less powerful and successful it looks to the rest of the world. So what happens if foreign countries stop buying U.S. Treasury bonds? Where would the money necessary to fund government operations and federal programs be borrowed from then? That is a difficult question to answer because the only way the United States can make money is to sell bonds and securities and/or raise taxes.

The challenge of managing debt is a huge one, and the more deficit spending that is done, the deeper the country will go into debt. The danger of bankruptcy always lurks whenever debt is taken on. Bankruptcy occurs when an individual, company, institution, or government is declared by law to be unable to repay its debts. A country edges close to bankruptcy when it can pay only the interest on the loan and not have enough left over to pay down the principal (the original loan amount itself).

MYTHS and FACTS

MYTH A nation with a balanced budget does not have debt.

FACT A balanced budget does not necessarily mean that the nation has paid off its preexisting debt. It does mean that it is not currently deficit spending, so the debt is not growing (except for accruing interest payments). A balanced budget is a positive move toward paying off the debt, but the task ahead is still huge. During the five years of budget surpluses under President Bill Clinton, the nation was still trillions of dollars in debt.

MYTH If a nation becomes bankrupt, it has no money at all.

FACT The word "bankrupt" refers to a legal declaration that a person, company, or nation cannot pay outstanding debts. A nation may declare bankruptcy to save itself from having to use its available funds to pay off creditors first. Once declared bankrupt, the debt can be restructured and the government can begin paying it down while still funding its operations and programs.

MYTH A nation in the midst of a recession must use deficit spending to pay for its programs.

FACT It is very difficult to balance a budget during a time of financial recession, but it is not impossible. Cuts in spending can help a nation avoid large deficits that may only slow or drag down any long-term economic recovery.

CHAPTER FOUR

THE UNITED STATES— CONSUMER AND PRODUCER

If you inspect the tags sewn inside the clothing you wear or turn over various items in your home, you may find information that tells you where these items were made. More and more items that are bought and sold today are made in countries other than the United States (even when the companies that make them are American). Many are made in China and other countries that manufacture goods, such as Thailand, India, and Japan.

AMERICA'S PAST MANUFACTURING MIGHT

This was not always the case, however. The United States used to manufacture and produce on American soil most of the goods that it bought and sold. Starting at the beginning of the Industrial Revolution in the late eighteenth and early nineteenth centuries, factories sprung up around the United States to create the goods that the country needed. Factories

The United States used to manufacture a lot of its own goods, but today China is the largest manufacturer of products bought by Americans.

in Michigan built the parts that assembled the cars Americans drove. The very idea of an assembly line was invented in the United States by Henry Ford and later put to use by other companies to make countless consumer items. Many American companies that we know today started during the first half of the twentieth century, when manufacturing was the major component of the nation's economy.

Factories put many people to work around the country. One factory in a rural town could employ most of the townspeople. The employees would get a paycheck from an American company and pay taxes to the U.S. government to help pay for the country's expenses. The salary the workers earned was spent at local businesses, and those businesses also paid taxes to the government. And the goods that were produced at the factories provided the products the country needed to be a growing and thriving nation.

Manufacturing Goes Overseas

Today, however, a lot of the manufacturing and factory work of American-owned companies is performed in foreign countries. Why has this happened?

Simply put, the cost of paying American workers is a large expense for many companies. Corporations came to realize that workers in other countries could do the same work for a lot less pay. If the American company had the same work done elsewhere for less, it would enjoy larger profits. It would also be able to charge less for the product so that more people would buy it.

As a result, many American workers were put out of work. Since the 1950s, there has been a steady decline in the amount of manufacturing that is done in the United States. In more recent years, the decline has happened more quickly than ever. Many factories remain empty, have been torn down, or have been converted into other types of buildings.

While the outsourcing of manufacturing overseas was originally meant to boost the profits of American companies, it ended up negatively affecting the economy of the United States. Many American workers trained to work in the factories found

Many American factories that once produced goods are now closed down or used for other purposes, such as housing or artists' studios.

themselves chronically unemployed and lacking in skills and training to perform any other kind of job. When the unemployment rate rose, less money was earned in tax revenues. As a result, the state and federal governments also suffered the effects of corporate America's decision to outsource production and labor.

IMPORTS, EXPORTS, TRADE DEFICITS, AND OUTSOURCING

The word "export" refers to the goods made in one's own country that are sold to other countries. The word "import" refers to the goods that are made by other countries and brought into one's own country to be sold to consumers and businesses. In recent years, the amount of goods that the United States exports has been less than the amount of goods that it imports. This means it buys more foreign goods than it sells American goods abroad, and the result is a trade deficit.

A trade deficit is bad for the American economy. The money that American workers earn and then spend on foreign goods goes to countries other than ours. These foreign countries become richer and can

Cars used to be one of America's major exports when U.S. manufacturing might was second to none. Nowadays, however, scrap metal—much of it from rusting junked cars—is the United States' largest export material.

afford to compete with the United States, making and selling even more goods at lower and lower prices. American goods become more expensive, both at home and abroad, and therefore go unsold. American companies make fewer profits, they lay off American workers, and federal tax revenue from corporations, businesses, and individuals decreases. Deficit spending and debt are the inevitable outcome.

During the twentieth century, the main U.S. exports included cars, metals, foods, tobacco, and electrical equipment. Today, not only are more Americans buying foreign cars, but even so-called American cars are partially made overseas to keep the manufacturing costs down. Most electronic equipment is made in other countries. Metal factories overseas now make and sell far more products than does the United States. All of these factors increase the U.S. trade deficit, threaten American jobs, and, ultimately, increase budget deficits and the debt load.

Outsourcing can intensify these economic pressures. A worker in China or India may make just a few dollars a day for his or her work. American workers are required by law to make at least $7 an hour, and in some states this amount may be even more. Compared to a Chinese worker, that sounds like a lot more money, but $7 will buy a lot less in the United States than it would in China. Minimum wage allows no American worker an extravagant lifestyle. In fact, if a minimum-wage salary is that worker's sole source of income, he or she will be living well below the poverty line.

Still, American companies often find even the minimum wage to be unacceptably high, so they hire far cheaper foreign labor and shift operations overseas. The effect is higher

American unemployment, decreased consumer spending, and lower tax revenue. These, in turn, result in state and federal budget deficits and deeper debt. The end result is that the U.S. economy has become weaker, while the economies of other nations have become stronger.

NEW IDEAS FOR RESTARTING AMERICAN MANUFACTURING

Politicians and government officials understand that it is important to revitalize manufacturing in the United States so that the nation can again begin to produce more goods. This would increase the self-sufficiency of the American economy and provide a spur to exports and sales of American-made goods abroad. It would also help provide more jobs for Americans and raise more tax revenue to close budget deficits and pay off the rising national debt.

The United States is still strong in many areas of manufacturing, product development, research, and exporting. Many ideas for high-tech products are developed in the United States. Scientists in American labs do a lot of important research. Development of new products, such as medicine and medical technologies, is done in the United States as well. Fashion, design, and entertainment are fields that are dominated by American ideas, creators, talent, companies, and products. Even when American clothing is manufactured overseas, more profits go to the company that designed the product than manufactured it.

Still, there has been a major shift in the American economy over the last fifty years that the United States and its workers are still adjusting to. The American workforce does not produce

Faster, Lighter, Thinner

Cameras and Gyro

iOS 4.3 + FaceTime & Photo

iMovie & GarageBand ($4.9

65,000 iPad apps

The United States is still a leader in high-tech product development, but many of these products, like the Apple iPad, are manufactured overseas to cut costs and boost profits.

as many actual goods as it once did. While American workers still construct buildings and are skilled laborers, many of the supplies they need to do the job are manufactured overseas. Most economists agree that, in addition to curbing spending, the United States should make revitalizing American manufacturing a priority if it wants to fix the problem of national debt and deficit spending. The more American jobs that are created and the more American products that are developed and sold, the more money that can be raised by the federal government. The government could then fund the operations and programs that benefit all Americans, without having to raise the taxes of all Americans.

THE IMPORTANCE OF TRADE RELATIONSHIPS

Revitalizing American manufacturing is not as simple a process as it sounds, however. Remember that American workers require much more money than foreign workers to perform the same job. The extra labor expenses must be paid by the company making the goods. Some companies could not afford to do that.

Assuming a company is not willing to accept lower profits, the higher labor costs get passed on to consumers, who pay more for the product that the American workers produced. Think about the cost of an iPhone, which costs hundreds of American dollars. While the product is made by an American company, it is manufactured in China, where the cost of skilled labor is a lot lower. If the same phone were made in the United States, it might cost thousands of dollars to buy instead of hundreds. Either the product would be too expensive for the vast majority of people to be able to afford, or the company would not be able to make a profit by making and selling the phone at a price that was affordable to average consumers.

Another important thing to consider about foreign manufacturing is the relationships that the United States has forged with its foreign trade partners. The United States has come to rely on its good relations with China, India, and other nations. It took many often rocky decades to develop some of these friendly trade relations. Suddenly changing them in order to

By maintaining friendly relations with our trade partners and providing manufacturing work to their citizens, the U.S. government and American-owned companies help ensure that foreign consumers will continue to purchase American products.

provide a boost to domestic manufacturing would not only be costly to American companies that had been using overseas labor, but would also cause America's trade partners economic problems of their own.

That would put the United States into an awkward position with many of its trade partners. And some of these trade partners are also the United States' creditors, having purchased American debt in the form of Treasury bonds. On the one hand, the United States relies on other nations to make American products affordable by manufacturing them inexpensively with cheap foreign labor. On the other hand, foreign nations rely on the United States to help provide work for their own citizens. This is a delicate symbiotic relationship that can't be altered without the danger of great harm and pain for all concerned.

CHAPTER FIVE

GETTING OUT OF DEBT

It is clear to most Americans that something must be done to pay down the national debt and reduce deficit spending. The federal government is working hard to propose ideas that can receive the support of both political parties and help fix the situation.

TAXES AND SPENDING CUTS

Raising taxes, especially for the top 1 percent of American earners, has been discussed a lot. The money brought in by this ultra-wealthy class would help raise billions of dollars each year. However, critics of the idea say that these high earners are the very people who are in the best position to create new American investments, companies, and jobs. If they are forced to pay more taxes, they may not be able to afford to put as much of their money back into the economy.

Another idea is to drastically reduce spending. Both the federal and the state governments are looking for items in

Reducing the debt means reducing spending on many important programs. NASA is one of the federal agencies that has been hard hit by budget cuts. With its funding slashed and mandate unclear, NASA's future is highly uncertain, especially following the end of the space shuttle program.

their budgets to cut. Funding cuts for the arts, public broadcasting, the space program, and scholarships are all being proposed. However, any national budget must be approved by many committees and be voted on by members of Congress. This is done to make sure that the budget decisions represent the will of a majority of the American people, or rather that of the politicians who claim to represent them. There are so many ideas in circulation about what should be cut from the federal budget that it is hard to find consensus on any one of them. Cutting the budget is a difficult thing to do because any one cut is bound to negatively affect the lives of many Americans.

Lessons from Germany

Germany is the only nation that experienced economic growth during the most recent global recession. One of the main reasons why it did not suffer as much as the rest of the world is that it did not enter the recession with a large debt load. It also emphasized exports, providing for high revenues and relatively high employment.

To further support employment rates, the German government set up a system called work sharing. A German company that is forced to reduce its workforce in a troubled economy does not lay off a percentage of its employees, as companies routinely do in other countries. Instead, German companies reduce the hours of all the workers. Meanwhile, the government agrees to compensate employees for any lost work hours. This way, people keep their jobs, maintain a steady income, and continue to pay taxes. In most cases, the money paid by the government to workers who have had their hours reduced is considerably less than what the government would have to pay in unemployment benefits if those same workers were laid off instead.

If a work share system had existed in the United States, it may have saved millions of people's jobs, prevented millions of home foreclosures, and allowed millions of families to stay afloat. It would have allowed steady tax revenue to continue to be collected by the government, enabling the funding of important stimulus and social programs without the need to engage in deficit spending.

While it is true that the German government would not be in a position to pay off its debt while funding the work share program

58

in the depths of the recession, it avoided going still deeper into debt. Because it kept employees working, receiving their normal wages, and paying their usual taxes, Germany avoided the fate of most other industrialized nations during the recession. Those countries went into ever deeper debt by increasing welfare spending in a period of sharply curtailed tax revenue.

Germany used a system called work sharing during the Great Recession of 2007–09. It kept more people employed, like this woman working in an Adidas factory, and kept the government from paying out large sums in unemployment benefits.

PRIVATIZATION

One idea that is often proposed along with spending cuts is the privatization of some government agencies. Privatization means that a public agency is sold to a private company. The national government is in charge of so many different agencies

Many Americans, especially older ones, feel that Social Security must be kept for the protection of the retired and elderly and not be viewed as a tempting target for deficit and debt reduction.

that it has become costly and overwhelming to manage them all. Managing all of the government agencies means paying employees, offering them costly insurance and benefits, and providing offices for them to work in and office equipment and supplies for them to use.

While it is good that public agencies create jobs, these jobs are also expensive to the government (and, therefore, to taxpayers). It has been proposed that some of these agencies be handled by private companies instead of the government itself. The main goals and mission of the agency would remain the same, but the government would no longer be in charge of paying for its staffing and operations.

Social Security

The U.S. Social Security Administration is the agency most often discussed as a possible agency to privatize. Because so many baby boomers will soon be retiring and drawing on Social Security insurance, many younger workers worry that there will be no Social Security money left for them to use when they retire. If the agency were privatized, the problem of a potential shortfall may be solved.

A private investment firm would pay a large sum of money to the government and take over the SSA's responsibilities. The government could use this money to pay down the national debt and/or close its budget deficit. In addition, the

The Transportation Security Administration (TSA) is a federal agency that is often viewed as a good candidate for privatization. Yet the ensuing cost savings to the federal government may be offset by serious concerns over national security and citizen privacy and safety.

government would no longer have the obligation of making Social Security payments every month and budgeting for them. The payments would instead come from a private company.

As with any other major change in government policies, there are risks and consequences. The current Social Security system is set up to provide reliable payments to citizens who are over a certain age. If the agency is privatized, the same rules may not apply. Perhaps the company operating Social Security would raise the retirement age or lower monthly benefits. Citizens may have more freedom to invest their Social Security money the way they wish in a private system. While this could mean that they may be able to make more money, they also have the potential of losing their money with bad investments or during economic downturns.

THE DEPARTMENT OF EDUCATION

The Department of Education is another U.S. agency that has been discussed as possibly being suited to privatization. If this came to pass, it would change the way schools are managed.

Currently, public schools are funded by federal and state money. The federal government recently issued a set of learning standards that are expected to be met by all students in the country at each grade level. Before that, it had been up to each state to devise its own standards for student learning. If the Department of Education were sold to a private company, it would then be that company, not the government, that would be in charge of

63

making sure that students learned what they were supposed to at each grade level.

One possible benefit to privatization is that a private company may be able to offer teachers better pay than they currently receive. It is unlikely, however, that a private company would allow teachers to unionize. Therefore, contract elements like salaries and salary increases, benefits, and tenure would be revised and possibly stripped. In addition, if the private company were operating schools in the hopes of making a profit, it might be tempted to cut corners and slash spending on important items like computers, books, and library resources. Another potential drawback would be that the money to pay for the schools would likely have to come directly from the families of the students, possibly in the form of tuition, and not from the federal and state governments (and ultimately from taxpayers). This may make some families unable to afford an education for their children.

TRANSPORTATION SECURITY ADMINISTRATION

Another agency often discussed for privatization is the Transportation Security Administration (TSA). This agency is part of the U.S. Department of Homeland Security. It was founded in 2001 after the September 11 terrorist attacks on the United States. The agency is responsible for protecting the nation's transportation systems by, among other things, looking for bombs at checkpoints in airports, inspecting rail cars, patrolling subways, and working to make all modes of transportation safe.

The agency employs many inspectors who work at airports screening passengers and baggage before they board airplanes.

The equipment used to do the scanning has become more and more elaborate and expensive since the agency first started. Some politicians propose privatizing the agency so that these rising costs would not have to be borne by the government.

However, this would also mean that the government might not have direct and immediate access to any counterterrorism information gathered by the agency. As a result, it may not be able to respond as quickly to threats and other situations revealed through the intelligence gathered by the private company. A potentially tragic delay between notification and action could occur. In addition, the private company, not the government, would have the power to decide which citizens are screened, how they are screened, and what will be looked for during these screenings.

As with any private company, the goal is to make a profit. That's why privatizing any agency, such as Welfare Services, the Department of Education, Medicare, or Medicaid, would possibly put profits before the ideals of public service that these agencies were founded upon. However, with the ever-increasing budget deficits and national debt, the government is looking at as many options as possible for cutting spending.

Ten Great Questions
to Ask a Financial Adviser

1 How can I save money during a recession?

2 What are the effects of the national debt and deficit spending on a family's financial situation?

3 How much interest would I earn if I bought a savings bond?

4 How long does it take for savings bonds to mature and earn interest?

5 What can I do if I want to buy something during an inflationary period?

6 How can a person or family draw up and stick to a budget?

7 How can I tell where my taxes are going?

8 Can an individual with a lot of debt declare bankruptcy?

9 What do the Federal Reserve's actions have to do with my own personal finances?

10 How can I reduce my own spending to avoid taking on debt, similar to the way a government does?

GLOSSARY

bankruptcy A legal declaration that a person or organization cannot pay its outstanding debts.

bond A certificate issued by a government or company that promises to repay borrowed money with interest.

budget An estimate of what will be earned and what will be spent during a certain period.

creditor A person, company, or other group that money is owed to.

debt Money that is owed to another person or group after it has been borrowed.

deficit The amount that is spent over the amount that is earned.

deficit spending Expenditures that exceed the amount taken in as revenue by a group, such as a government; spending more money than has been collected and is available.

exports The goods that are made by a particular country and that are then shipped and sold overseas.

Federal Reserve The central bank of the United States; it manages the nation's money supply and oversees its banks.

imports Foreign-manufactured goods that are brought into a country for sale.

inflation An increase in the cost of goods and services.

Medicaid A health program for families and individuals with low incomes.

Medicare A public insurance program for citizens over sixty-five years of age and for citizens of any age with certain disabilities.

privatize When a public, governmental agency is sold to and operated by a private enterprise.

recession An economic downturn, usually defined as six months or more of declining value of a nation's goods and services. A recession is typically characterized by unemployment, low consumer and business spending, and a lack of money circulating throughout the economy.

revenue The income of a company or government during a certain period of time.

Social Security A government insurance program that helps provide financial assistance to the unemployed, retired, and disabled.

tax Money that is paid to a government from workers' incomes, business profits, or the cost of goods and services in order to fund government operations and programs to the benefit of all citizens.

Treasury securities Government debt issued by the U.S. government; investors who buy these securities (including foreign nations) receive their original investment back, plus interest, after a certain period of time.

FOR MORE INFORMATION

Board of Governors of the Federal Reserve System
20th Street and Constitution Avenue NW
Washington, DC 20551
Web site: http://www.federalreserve.gov
The Federal Reserve is the central bank of the United
    States.

Bureau of Economic Analysis (BEA)
1441 L Street NW
Washington, DC 20230
(202) 606-9900
Web site: http://www.bea.gov
Part of the Department of Commerce, the BEA produces
    accounts statistics on the American economy.

Canadian Economics Association (CEA)
CP 8888 Succ. Centre-Ville
Montréal, QC H3C 3P8
Canada
(514) 987-3000, ext. 8374
Web site: http://economics.ca
The CEA is an organization of about 1,500 economists in
    Canada.

Department of Finance Canada
140 O'Connor Street
Ottawa, ON K1A0G5
Canada
(613) 992-1573
Web site: http://www.fin.gc.ca
The Department of Finance oversees the Canadian
    government's budget and spending.

Jump$tart Coalition for Personal Financial Literacy
919 18th Street NW, Suite 300
Washington, DC, 20006
(888) 45-EDUCATE (453-3822)
Web site: http://www.jumpstart.org
The Jump$tart Coalition is a nonprofit partnership of many
    national organizations that support financial education
    or provide tools for teaching financial education.

Junior Achievement
1 Education Way
Colorado Springs, CO 80906
(719) 540-8000
Web site: http://www.ja.org
Junior Achievement is the world's largest organization for
    educating students about financial literacy through
    hands-on programs.

National Council on Economic Education (NCEE)
122 East 42nd Street, Suite 2600
New York, NY 10168

(212) 730-7007
Web site: http://www.councilforeducation.org
The NCEE is a nationwide network that promotes economic
    literacy for students and their teachers.

National Economists Club
P.O. Box 19281
Washington, DC 20036
(703) 493-8824
Web site: http://www.national-economists.org
The National Economists Club is a nonprofit, nonpartisan
    organization with the goal of encouraging and sponsoring
    discussion and an exchange of ideas on economic trends
    and issues that are relevant to public policy.

National Endowment for Financial Education (NEFE)
1331 17th Street, Suite 1200
Denver, CO 80202
(303) 741-6333
Web site: http://www.nefe.org
The NEFE is a national nonprofit foundation dedicated to
    helping Americans control their own finances.

Office of Management and Budget (OMB)
725 17th Street NW
Washington, DC 20503
(202) 395-3080
Web site: http://www.whitehouse.gov/omb
Among other duties, the OMB develops and executes the
    federal budget and manages federal agencies.

U.S. Department of the Treasury
1500 Pennsylvania Avenue NW
Washington, DC 20220
(202) 622-2000
Web site: http://www.treas.gov
The Department of the Treasury's mission is to maintain a
strong economy and create economic and job
opportunities by promoting the conditions that enable
economic growth and stability at home and abroad;
strengthen national security by combating threats and
protecting the integrity of the financial system; and
manage the U.S. government's finances and resources
effectively.

WEB SITES

Due to the changing nature of Internet links, Rosen Publishing
has developed an online list of Web sites related to the subject
of this book. This site is updated regularly. Please use this link
to access the list:

http://www.rosenlinks.com/rwe/def

FOR FURTHER READING

Acton, Johnny, and David Goldblatt. *Economy*. New York, NY: DK, 2010.

Andrews, Carolyn. *Economics in Action*. New York, NY: Crabtree Publishing, 2008

Craats, Rennay. *Economy: USA Past Present Future*. New York, NY: Weigl Publishers, 2009.

Fradin, Dennis Brindell, and Judith Bloom Fradin. *Borrowing*. Tarrytown, NY: Marshall Cavendish, 2010.

Gale Group. *The U.S. Economy*. Farmington Hills, MI: Gale Cengage Learning, 2010.

Gorman, Tom. *The Complete Idiot's Guide to the Great Recession*. New York, NY: Penguin Group, 2010.

Hall, Alvin. *Show Me the Money: How to Make Cents of Economics*. New York, NY: DK, 2008.

Jewler, Sue. *Making Sense of Economics*. Hawthorne, NJ: Educational Impressions, 2006.

Merino, Noel. *The World Economy* (Current Controversies). San Diego, CA: Greenhaven Press, 2010.

Miller, Debra A. *The U.S. Economy* (Current Controversies). San Diego, CA: Greenhaven Press, 2010.

Murphy, Patricia. *Earning Money*. Berkeley Heights, NJ: Lerner Publishing Group, 2006.

Thomas, Lloyd B. *The Financial Crisis and Federal Reserve Policy*. New York, NY: Palgrave Macmillan, 2011.

BIBLIOGRAPHY

Bonner, William, and Addison Wiggin. *The New Empire of Debt*. Hoboken, NJ: John Wiley & Sons, Inc., 2009.

Brain, Marshall. "What Is the National Debt Per Person in the United States?" HowStuffWorks.com, February 27, 2009. Retrieved February 2011 (http://blogs. howstuffworks.com/2009/02/27/good-question-what-is-the-national-debt-per-person-in-the-united-states).

Cavanaugh, Francis X. *The Truth About the National Debt: Five Myths and One Reality*. Cambridge, MA: Harvard Business School Press, 1996.

China IT Online. "How Much Cheaper Is It to Have All Your Manufacturing Done in China Compared to the U.S.?" August 8, 2009. Retrieved February 2011 (http:// www.chinaitproducts.com/how-much-cheaper-is-it-to-have-all-your-manufacturing-done-in-china-compared-to-the-us).

eHow.com. "How Does a Treasury Bond Work?" Retrieved February 2011 (http://www.ehow.com/how-does_4685111_treasury-bond-work.html).

Hagenbaugh, Barbara. "U.S. Manufacturing Jobs Fading Away Fast." *USA Today*, December 12, 2002. Retrieved February 2011 (http://www.usatoday.com/money/economy/2002-12-12-manufacture_x.htm).

Kinkade, Brian. "Greece Makes Big Plans for Repaying Its National Debt." Real Estate Industry Watch, January 29, 2011. Retrieved February 2011 (http://realestateindustrywatch.com/greece-makes-big-plans-for-repaying-its-national-debt).

O'Keefe, Ed. "2011 Budget: Spending Cuts and Reductions." *Washington Post*, February 1, 2010. Retrieved February 2011 (http://voices.washingtonpost.com/federal-eye/2010/02/2011_budget_spending_cuts_and.html).

Paulson, Amanda. "Which States Are Facing the Worst Budget Deficits in 2010?" *Christian Science Monitor*, December 30, 2009. Retrieved February 2011 (http://www.csmonitor.com/USA/2009/1230/Which-states-are-facing-the-worst-budget-deficits-in-2010).

Schoen, John W. "U.S. Budget Deficit Fix: Print More Money?" MSNBC.com, October 1, 2004. Retrieved February 2011 (http://www.msnbc.msn.com/id/7089510/ns/business-answer_desk).

Swanson, Gerald J. *America the Broke: How the Reckless Spending of the White House and Congress Are Bankrupting Our Country and Destroying Our Children's Future*. New York, NY: Random House, 2004.

Thompson, Derek. "3 Things to Learn from the German Economy, and 3 Things Not To." *Atlantic*, September 9, 2010. Retrieved February 2011 (http://www.theatlantic.com/business/archive/2010/09/3-things-to-learn-from-the-german-economy-and-3-things-not-to/62678).

USGovernmentSpending.com. "Federal Debt as Pct GDP." Retrieved February 2011 (http://www.

usgovernmentspending.com/downchart_
gs.php?title=Federal%20Debt%20as%20Pct%20
GDP&year=1950_2010&chart=H0-fed&units=p).

U.S. Treasury. "Major Foreign Holders of Treasury Securities."
March 15, 2011. Retrieved March 2011 (http://www.
treasury.gov/resource-center/data-chart-center/tic/
Documents/mfh.txt).

Wiggin, Addison, and Kate Incontrera. *I.O.U.S.A.: One
Nation. Under Stress. In Debt.* Hoboken, NJ: John Wiley
& Sons, Inc., 2008.

Wright, Robert E. *One Nation Under Debt: Hamilton, Jefferson,
and the History of What We Owe.* New York, NY:
McGraw-Hill, New York, NY: 2008.

INDEX

ABOUT THE AUTHORS

Kathy and Adam Furgang have written extensively about economics and government, including books on the stock market, economic indicators, the Seventh and Ninth Amendments to the U.S. Constitution, and an entire series on the Declaration of Independence and its signers. They live in Colonie, New York.

PHOTO CREDITS

Cover (debt clock), p. 1 (bottom right) Chris Hondros/Getty Images; cover (headline) © www.istockphoto.com/Lilli Day; pp. 6, 19, 30–31, 38–39, 59 Bloomberg/Bloomberg via Getty Images: pp. 9, 21, 34, 44, 56 from photo by Mario Tama/Getty Images; p. 11 English School/The Bridgeman Art Library/Getty Images; p. 13 © AP Images; p. 14 R. Gates/Archive Photos/Getty Images; p. 16 Buyenlarge/Archive Photos/Getty Images; p. 22–23 Yuri Cortez/AFP/Getty Images; pp. 26–27 Mandel Ngan/AFP/Getty Images; p. 29 Shutterstock; p. 35 Karen Blier/AFP/Getty Images; pp. 40–41 © AP Images; p. 45 Shutterstock; pp. 46–47, 60–61 Spencer Platt/Getty Images; pp. 48–49 Henry Horenstein/Photographer's Choice/Getty Images; p. 52 AFP/APF via Getty Images; p. 54 Mike Clarke/AFP/Getty Images; p. 57 NASA; pp. 62–63 John Moore/Getty Images; cover and interior graphic elements: © www.istockphoto.com/Andrey Prokhorov (front cover), © www.istockphoto.com/Dean Turner (back cover and interior pages); www.istockphoto.com/Darja Tokranova (p. 43); www.istockphoto.com/articular (p. 66); © www.istockphoto.com/studiovision (pp. 67, 69, 73, 74, 77); © www.istockphoto.com/Chen Fu Soh (multiple interior pages).

Designer: Nicole Russo, Photo Researcher: Marty Levick